Fourteen Eighty-Five
& Other Poems

by

J.A. Bosworth

To
all my children, grandchildren,
great-grandchildren, their partners
and successors.

Contents

Hawk

I saw a hunting hawk today, over
Near fields, on trembling feathers hanging high;
And marvelled at the link of brain to limb
Which gave such perfect mastery of flight:
    Until it stone-dropped suddenly from view,
Then rose again, triumphantly, above
The fringing *boscage* trailing, in clasped feet,
The abject object of its taloned stoop.
    The power and precision of that bird,
Whose keen eyes and compactly-muscled force
Co-ordinated so supernally,
Evoked that admiration in my mind
    Which is reserved for graceful artistry combined
    With purposeful executive facility!.

The Fox

As one, the fox and I were motionless.
Along the cool, sun-dappled path between
Tall-colonnaded trees – his tawny fur
Glistening with points of golden light, his dark
Eyes starred with bright intelligence; sharp-nosed,
White-toothed, pink tongue a-loll, inquisitive,
Relaxed and confident – he grinned at me.
    We stood there, calm and still, not twenty feet
Apart, as I returned a friendly smile,
Content to share this moment of *détente*:
Until my pair of dogs gambolled in view
And, at their coming, broke our mutual trust.
    With one last glance, which signalled dignified reproach,
    My fox faded into the unkempt undergrowth.

<u>The Aims of Art</u>

(from: *Neknus*, Canto XXV)

The aims of Art, in all its modes, should be
Chiefly to please and, with inspired effect,
Bring new understanding to those who seek.
Fine Art has always seemed to us to be
Symbolic of our highest intellect.
It draws us back from those commercial tasks
Which stultify the brain, and gives delight
To us when, in our leisured ease, we both
Mind and imagination may engage
Appreciating all the subtleties
Applied by craftsmen, to their first designs,
In order to perfect their final forms.
Whether they work in marble or in stone,
In clay, or glass, or clanging metalware;
Extract from sounding instruments rare tones;
Or on a silent surface make their marks,
With inks or paints of variegated hues:
Artistic hands – revealing mighty minds
And wonderful concepts – mysteriously
Have wrought their skilful monuments to Time,
Illuminating what had otherwise
Remained enveloped in obscurity.
Our visionary minds have always sought
New shapes, new textures or new sounds, for each
Imagined notion of our active brains,
No matter how abstruse. So, through our Art,
We can enlarge upon experience –
Giving reality to ageless dreams –
Helping our fellows to identify
With them, and share in our discoveries.

Spring Returns

Now that wild Winter's frenzied blasts have blown
        Their last, loud roar;
And frost and snow and bitterness have flown
        Away once more:
    Now is it time for lusty Spring
            To sport
    Amidst long-hibernated thought
            And bring
Its happy urgency, so long unknown.

Fresh flowerlets on every side appear
        To flaunt their plumes
In light abandon, now that they need fear
        Not Winter's glooms:
    And fledgelings and young creatures wake
            To see
    Around them charmed felicity
            Now make
The world so pleasant, that was so severe.

Innocent love, in Spring, absorbs the hearts
        Of man and maid;
In many secludedly private parts
        Sweet games are played
    As scalds the hot blood in their veins
            Still more;
    Nor he nor her thinks to be sure,
            But strains
To reach perfection through romantic arts.

Of the four Seasons comprising the year
        Winter is crude;
Plague-smitten Autumn is saddest, I fear;
        Rich Summer good:

But Spring's eternal enchantments
        Must be
Adjudged far better than these three.
        Spring lends
The Earth a loveliness beyond compare.

The Pool

Step into the Pool, my darling.
        (Do not be afraid!).
Let its waters close about you
        Like a fond embrace.
Totally immerse your being
        In its lustrous depths;
Give yourself to its calm comfort:
        Gently, then, relax!.
Here there is no need for worry;
        Here no cause for doubt:
For these waters of contentment –
        Set for you apart –
Are the deep-distilled affections
        Of my loving heart!.

The Old Woman

Frail as winter twigs she goes;
        As tremblant, too!.
Pale eyes peer blankly down thin nose;
        Shuffles each shoe.
Age holds her in its palsied thrall,
        Infirm and slow;
Fitful faint memories are all
        She now can know!.
Impatient for her dragging time
        To end, she needs

Warm-hearted kindness, and love's breath,
        To bring her ease
Along that certain, gradual decline
Which leads into the doubtful dark of death.

Ireland

Through fresh green fields and orchards ran
The road he had to tread;
Through straggled towns and villages
        His path of duty led.
Till in some place he did not know –
Although it *seemed* he knew –
He saw the One he thought he'd meet
        Before his task was through
Standing nearby, in silhouette,
Against the troubled sky.
So he approached and calmly spoke
        Those words he had to say:
"To Ireland's aid I have been sent;
To Ireland I have come!".
The One replied: "I give you Peace"
        And turned him eyes which shone.
Welcoming his caught breath
He recognised the face…of Death!.

Lest You Rue

Do not linger, lucky maid;
        Go with him
Who for your heart has prayed,
    For see, he loves you!.
Do not proudly stand aloof,
        Nor seek from him

Too much proof
　　As a final token,
For his heart has spoken!.
　　Take him,
　While you may,
Lest you rue this day!.

Winter Gales

Those galling gales, which in rough Winter rush
Across bald-headed mountaintops exposed
To their wild buffetings as captives to
Some hateful prison-master's vicious scourge:
　Over the cringing, wooded-hillsides' slopes
They violently hasten with rude roars,
Like raging sea-surges pounding rock shores
Intemperately.
　　　　　All the laggard leaves
They lash from fear-chilled branches tossed in fright
At such loud-voiced disparagement. Down through
Lush valleys' huddling fields they storm towards
Wide-open plains impatiently, flogging
Fast-fading petals from the latest flowers
Which dare to flaunt their lingering delights
In wanton display; whipping thin hedgerows
With undisguised *chagrin* to find them still
Dissenting from predestined dominance.
　Swift scurriers of ice-eyed Winter's cold
Autocracy, bearing its messages
Of glacial control, their frenzied zeal
In executing such commissions seems
Immoderate.
　　　　Although we know that Spring
Could not revivify the world without
This purging of degeneration's dross,
Each Winter gale resembles, in its force,
That bigot passion which, unbridled, drives

Through ruthless human hearts when they pursue
The hapless victims of some demagogue;
Or implement, for personal reward,
Dark deeds of wickedness by others schemed.
　　It is the fate of sycophants to be
Reviled for acts their masters urge them to:
But those who serve a tyrant's will or whim
Deserve their disrepute, however grim.

Global Warfare

Day's light battalions withdraw towards the West
　Surrendering each field and hill, reluctantly,
　　Beneath the heavy-cavalry attacks which mark
　　　The front line of another battle in their war,
　　(Which has no ending in recorded history),
　Against oppressive, ultimate obscurity.
Descending from the East, the hordes of night advance
　Dark phalanx upon phalanx dark. Retiring day
　　Observes their progress through etiolated stars
　　　Blenching among the nebulous cimmerities
　　Which occupy defenceless hills and vales with their
　Invading armies of pervasive nullity.
If I were not aware that, in dark's dust, dawn's vanguard-light
Closely pursued, then I would fear the onset of each night.

<u>**Naissance**</u>

I feel expectance in each sense,
(Not of some tragedy or ill,
Rather of pre-deliverance):
A turmoil of crescendent will.
I cannot ease this veiled unrest,
Nor make advance what it portends:
(Which run their courses as they must
Until their self-determined ends).
I, anxiously contented, wait
For this resolving flux to firm:
Part feared, part calm and part elate
To know the issue of its term
Which, in due time delivered, will surprise
Its parent-midwife's pre-conceived surmise!.

The Lover's Complaint

Love is a caring, sharing sentiment!.
 I do not want some smooth-wrought words writ down
To justify your lack of faith in me.
 I want to feel the *actions* of your love,
The *doing*, (not the *telling*!), of your heart's
 Emotions, unreserved and free from doubts.

I want your confidence and trust to shew
 In sharing with me *all* your life; not just
To let me have a 'special' *part* of you.

 Between two lovers there should not exist
One single separating secret thought
 Defining where they have no right to be.

So do not so distrust *yourself* that you can trust
Nobody else at all!. That's not true love for me.

Cooking the Books?

"Why rushed the discords in but that harmony should be
prized?"

(Abt Vogler. by R. Browning)

Perhaps we should not scorn those vulgar works
  Which often have offended our concern
    For purity and beauty; for what irks
  Our minds and brings some bitter taste to burn
The palates of our sensibilities
  May serve as complements to underline
    The subtler flavours which our method tries
  To cook into the poems we refine
With so much tender care. For it is sure
  That too much sweetness in a meal can be
    As disappointing as can too much sour:
  A contrast adds delectability.
So let them do their worst, those whom our own taste loathes;
We'll be the honey to their baked ham's acrid cloves!.

Night Force

Those 'Nights that brought [him] to her body bare'
  Could they not also strip his heart for her?
    What fuels his passion's consummating fires
  Could that not spark the words she so desires?
O those bare nights and that occluded heart,
(Pulled close by longing, by fear held apart),
  Could they not meld their feelings without thought
    To demonstrate their love without report?
  For she needs words of ecstasy not such
Acceptance of calm intellect's cool touch;
  And she asks ardour spiced with urgent speech
  To justify response to body's breach.

'The force that through the green fuze drives the flowers'
  Is not less strong in him than other lovers;
    Yet she wants florid words forced from his brain
  Though he is fearful of the inner pain –
Which might be caused to both of them – if he
Should loose love's wildness so abandonedly.
  Must care's discretion then spell tragedy?
    Should intimates reserve no modesty?
  Need passion be expressed through decadence
To abrogate his thoughtful reticence?
  Why be afraid to overwhelm her doubt?
  Why not use potent words to drive it out?

Those 'Nights that brought [him] to her body bare':
  That force which 'through the green fuze drives the flower';
  Could they not bare his heart as well for her delight?
Could they not drive his ardour through its groundless fright?

To Please My Sense

(Eriu – Ireland)

Coquette colleen! Such drear, dull clothes curtail
  Your splendours wrapping them behind a veil
    Of dropping, drooping, drab obscurity.
  What is it that you think to hide from me
By so encumbering my hopeful view?
  I know your attributes and I have seen
    Your secret places. You need not endue
  This overmantling vague opacity
To serve your privities as modest screen.
  Stop your dissembling: for you know I'm not
    So inexperienced an idiot
  As is seduced by such false prudery.
Discard this useless dress; wear confidence! You dare
More loveliness, to please my sense, when you are bare!.

Bath

(After a photograph)

Here is a structured question-mark. The gold
Great Crescent's elegant *façade* sweeps round
   To meet strait Brock Street's subfusc straight that guides
     Towards a perfect ornate roundel which,
       Lawned and tree-centred, forms the Circus; all
     Three elements harmoniously combined
   Into one interrogative design
Of architectural magnificence.
Why here, far from the Eastern capital
Of London's cosmopolitan huge wealth?
Why not in Bristol, prosperously large
Commercial harbour near the Western coast?

Because the Romans found at Bath a healing stream,
Or Georgian Society a scenic dream?.

Mortal Deeds, Immortal Needs

  Perhaps beside some sliding stream or on
More modish bed they move barely as one –
Senses in lightshine bathed or nightshade swathed –
Performing privately those ancient rites
Which tune emotions to shared harmonies,
Their interactions from profane eyes screened
By foliage of circumambient plants
Or other modest veilings of the site.
  In every generation such routines
Of life's most intimate activities
Are re-enacted on a world-wide scale

17

Innumerable times by countless pairs
   Unwittingly expressing in their mortal deeds
   Partial fulfilments of immortal human needs.

Islanders

O the islanders may love the sea
   When in its halcyon mood,
Since it's in their blood, for ill or good,
   As none knows better than they
     Their heart-enchanting sea.

Or the islanders may dread the sea
   Which keeps them from their darlings;
They may loathe its storms and sullen calms
   And the deep inconstancy
     Which moves their tameless sea.

But the islanders may hate the sea
   When in its dangerous mood,
Though it's in their blood, for ill or good,
   As none knows better than they
     Their cruel, remorseless sea.

Or the islanders may fight the sea –
   Its tides, waves, currents, weathers –
When the salty tangs upon their tongues
   Taste of sweat and blood to they
     In an aggressive sea.

But the islanders may sail the sea
   To travel, trade or sport there,
Since it's in their blood, for ill or good,
   Whatever their feelings be
     Towards their circling sea.

Or the islanders may farm the sea
    For all that it possesses
Though they little gain without the pain
    Of laboured persistency
        Amid the teeming sea.

O the islanders may love the sea
    Or dread, hate, fight, sail, farm it;
But it's in their blood, for ill or good,
    For so long as memory
        Reminds them of the sea –
            Their ever-changing sea.

Relativity

As streetlamps like small thin dawns revealing
    Through first pink flush of insect-fluttered glow
        Their little worlds' faint warm illuminings,
    Brightening the night with local radiance
And spreading heat and light around themselves:

    Just so throughout the pathless universe there roll
    Numerous nameless suns with their attendant worlds
Igniting, waxing, waning, burning out, which yet
    Are indiscernible or only faintly show
        At the dark timeless borders of expansive space

Cricket

(After L. Smart)

A village church-spire watching from nearby; a white,
Red-roofed pavilion shaded by trees. In front,
Upon a close-mown green some pale-clothed cricketers
Performing arcane rituals of Summer days
That mark their English heritage with bat and ball,
   With sandwiches and tea.
                     No need for crowds; no haste
   To settle scores within a frenzied hour or so.
Only the beauties of the ancient game: its style
And elegance, its blend of artistry and brawn,
Of spin and speed, of guile and force, of intermixed
Pleasures and pains and unpredictability
   Followed by evenings of conviviality.
Wherever Englishmen have made their homes abroad they've
                        brought
With them the quintessential character of this rare sport.

Tchaikovsky's Sixth Symphony

This last and greatest composition floods
   Emotions through the caverns of my sense
     As when high spring-tides swell to full expanse
   Of their majestic reach. All human moods
Are touchingly evoked through these deep themes
   Which thrill the ultimate extremes my mind
     Can apprehend. For in this work I find
   Compressed, and thus intensified like dreams,
Those strong sensations which make life to be
   So bitter-sweet for all of us: the calm
     Of satisfaction, glory's pride, the balm
   Of beauty, trust of hope, despair's *débris*
All blent together with such passion and such art
Tears spring from eyes burst by the fierce grasp of my heart.

A Poet's Magic Carpet?

(From: *A Theory for Art* [xix])

The weft and warp of poetry are wove
From sounds, alliteration, rhythmic beat,
Harmony, pattern, feeling; these strong threads
Are artfully combined by shuttle-thoughts,
Flying incessantly between, and bound
Into a comprehensive whole by knots
Of reason and imaginative flair.
Incorporated in this fabric-base
Are decorative elements designed
To illustrate it with sharp metaphors
And well-wrought, striking similes – coloured
Throughout by insight, humour, irony,
By paradox or natural, unforced
Ambiguous abstractions, as required
In due proportions for the poem's weight,
Its purpose and conceived significance –
  To serve the object of its maker's art:
  How best convey the poet's chosen theme.

The Greek Myths

(After reading Robert Graves's *The Greek Myths*)

i.
The Greek mythologers have given to the world,
(In stories of their great divinities and tales
Of heroes and of heroines almost as great
As whom they worshipped), such a treasure-house of art
And human understanding as can scarce be matched
From any other source of philosophic lore.
  Their comedies and tragedies, vulgarities
And wit, their wisdom and their learning were combined
With such felicitous, bold ingenuity

And subtle skill to colour with nobility,
Strong character and charm their nation's history
As made it universally applicable
To all States, times and cultures of humanity.

ii.

How then could you, grave Robert – being a confessed
Poet yourself, in thrall to that Great White Goddess
Who is your own self-honoured Muse – how then could you,
A poet, demythologise their timeless tales,
(By stripping off the fabric of their magic veils),
To leave them nakedly exposed as primitive
Crude cyphers of barbaric chieftains and their acts
Of stark political expedience and greed?
All are reduced to detailed footnotes, (erudite
It's true, but barren as the drought-plagued desert-wastes),
Which have murdered their vitality and displayed
Their bleached bones fleshless to the view of those who need
The inspiration which their beauty once bestowed.

iii.

The art of poets is to make, not mar, the force
Of inspiration's alchemy; to weave the web
Of magic, not unravel its alluring charms.
No doubt you honestly believed that in your book
The Greek Myths you were adding to their qualities
The extra gloss of authenticity – you meant
It for the best – but as a poet should have known
The path to Hades' Gorge is paved with good intents;
You should have let the stories keep their mysteries.
The ancient Greeks had euphemised with genius
Facts into fantasies more powerfully true
Than actuality itself; they knew their myths
Could teach more memorably than formal history.

iv.

Let lusty Zeus and jealous Hera rule their world
Untainted by corrosive pedantry; let Pan
Play his pert pipes and Orpheus his lyric lyre;

Let Aphrodite love and Heracles toil on;
Let all the Pantheon of high Olympus live
In wonted splendour and impetuosity!.
    They cannot do us harm who have our own beliefs
But, through the medium of their mythology,
They can enrich our lives' experience and shew,
(By that bright tapestry of tales which is their gift
To us), those basic truths which lie behind the words
    Of legendary yarns dramatically told
    To win the interest of all, both young and old.

Pride's Penalty

(15 March 44 BC)

Proud Caesar said: "The Ides of March are here!",
  Then asked: "Now where is he who prophesied
Great Julius this forecast time should fear?".

"The Ides are come", the prophet said: "Beware,
  Proud Consul, since their powers *yet* may chide".
Said Caesar: "These Ides mark nothing to fear!".

"What must be, will be", said the prophet: "Hear
  My words great Consul; humble your self-pride:
Great Julius this forecast time *should* fear!".

Scorned Caesar: "Your false prophesies I fleer!".
  Brutus, with Casca and their friends, beside
Proud Caesar smiled: "The Ides of March *are* here!".

Towards the Senate strode the group; but near
  Its entrance Caesar was surprised and knived
By those whom, in his pride, he did not fear.

The Consul rolled his fading eyes, (now blear
  With death's dull film), where Brutus stood astride.
Him. Caesar sighed: "The Ides of March *start* here!.

Brutus, my friend, you send me to my bier
  Upon whose loyalty I had relied.
This forecast time I was too *proud* to fear".

Brutus replied, mocking with cynic sneer
  The fate of one whose pride dismissed Fate's tide
Flooding his way: "The Ides of March *end* here!".

 But, as his body died, proud Caesar cried:
"The Ides of March are here; and I declare
False *Junius* this forecast time should fear!".
And with these words he turned his look aside.

[**Note**: Neither Julius Caesar nor Junius Brutus said the words attributed to them in this poem. Brutus was silent; but Caesar's reported 'famous last words', as he was assassinated, were not the reproachful "*Et tu, Brute!*" [**Latin**: 'You too, Brutus!'] – as I was taught in childhood – but the far more scornful "*Kai su, tekne!*" [**Greek**: 'You too, child!']; by which he may have meant that Brutus, a personal favourite and political *protégé*, was intellectually too immature and politically indecisive to govern Rome and its colonies successfully. It is also possible that Caesar intended to imply: 'This deed will also be the death of you, young man'. If so, the prophesy was realised at Philippi in 42 BC].

Dangerous Minds

'...the worst are full of passionate intensity'.
[W.B. Yeats: *The Second Coming*]

Zealots are dangerous. Their minds are closed
  About their sole enthusiastic cause:

Their bright eyes blind to contra-evidence,
Their keen ears deaf to counter-arguments.
Facts, logic, reason: these are all opposed
  With energumen bigotry because
    Such might discredit partisan appeal
    In those they would subvert to their ideal.
Zealots are narrow-minded, obstinate,
  Insolent activists who daren't allow
    Rational thought to moderate the spate
    Of their obsessed intensity. They know
Nothing of tolerance, of compromise, of sense;
Cynic determination their chief competence.

Immoderation

    The frantic thrusts of lust's long loin
Engender ill-considered fruits.
If we took thought to preconceive
The outcome of precipitance
We might become more temperate
And chaste in what we do inside
The darkened chambers of our minds
Behind the curtained eyes of haste.
    Passion is honourable when
It cedes to decency's demurs;
But when it forcibly insists
Incontinently to intrude,
Or have its way without restraint,
Upon its object of desire –
Like some wild-rutting animal –
The fathered offspring, raging hate,
    Will chase the shameful author of its wrath
    Till it achieves a vengeful aftermath.

<u>Aroona</u>

(Freshford, Somerset)

That lovely old house on the hill:
How grieved I was to lose her;
Sad beyond my telling
These memories welling
In me, as I picture her sunlit appeal

Smiling over the river, road,
Railway and tree-fringed canal;
Symbol past my telling
Of happiness swelling
In me, at *Aroona*, when she was my ward.

Proud over incline and village,
High above Church, Manor, Grange;
Quite beyond my telling
Those pleasures then welling
Through me, when her qualities were my hopes' gage.

Gracious lawns and gardens displayed
Flowers and cedar and pine:
Pleasures past my telling;
Now pining thoughts swelling
And spreading, like cedar, their flowerless shade.

Aroona has left my control:
Others enjoy her delights;
Now passed beyond telling
Those past hopes once welling
In me, for that lovely lost home on the hill.

Denominative Devices

You cannot live forever, no matter how you scheme;
The whole of your endeavour fades like a labile dream.
    But habits of your living
        Etch images in time,
    With history's page receiving
        Each graven paradigm.

What you create must sign you – each thing you make or do –
With memories to define you for those who never knew
    The pattern of your nature,
        The tenor of your heart,
    Or that unique self-signature
        Which marked your life apart.

Unless you leave some signs to shew you merit your recall,
So far as future minds will know, you had not lived at all.

The Wreck of the *Pelican*

    One day the *Pelican*
    From Bristol harbour ran,
Bound for the shores of tropic Africa.
    Aboard her there were ten,
    (Four women and six men),
Who journeyed with her; each a passenger.

    The weather, then, was calm;
    The breeze a salt-tanged balm
Wafting the grimy smoke clear of the deck.
    The turquoise-azure sea
    Was all tranquillity;
There were no portents, then, of tragic wreck.

    Soon out of sight was land;
    The waves on either hand

Heaved gently out, as far as eyes could see.
   As if in deep repose
   Smooth billows fell and rose:
Nothing disturbed the great solemnity;

   Save that the *Pelican*
   Before a fair wind ran,
Creaming a whorling furrow as she passed.
   The climate seemed to be
   In such sweet harmony
The playful zephyrs might forever last.

   For full twelve days she sailed,
   Whilst kindly winds prevailed,
Until Gibraltar was left far astern;
   But then, early next dawn,
   Dark clouds began to form
And gusty squalls the rising sea to churn.

   During that long day through
   The threatening cloud-hordes grew
Until they covered-over all the sky;
   Strong winds started to howl:
   Surly rough waves to growl
And fretfully toss spumy crests on high.

   That night a great storm smote,
   Seized on the fated boat
And shook her fiercely in its grasp of steel.
   As shock succeeded shock –
   Like hammers on a block –
She staggered in a crazy drunken reel.

   As every huge wave reared
   The passengers all feared
That moment to be cast into the sea;
   But, though out of control –
   Despite a frightful roll –
The *Pelican* would not yield easily.

Throughout that night she flew,
Whilst the wild storm-blasts blew,
Nearer the savage coast of Africa.
But just as frowned the dawn,
Bedraggled and forlorn,
She struck upon the reef that murdered her.

Then, through her riven side,
Swept in the roiling tide
Snatching at everything barring its way.
Though they fought boldly,
Yet they died coldly.
(Only three passengers got safe away).

All of her crew were lost,
Each one still at his post:
Dragged by the currents beneath ruthless waves;
Slowly they perished there,
Gasping for vital air:
Sternly courageous, they sank to their graves.

On the rough waters swirled
All that was left of her.
Mournfully tossing, amongst grim remains,
Just one frail raft survived
To succour three weak lives,
With one torn canvas to ward off the rains.

Numbed fingers, stiff and cold,
Maintained a frantic hold
On this poor craft as it writhed in the spume.
Pounded by breaking waves
They clasped the flimsy lathes,
Desperately battling a watery doom.

Two days they huddled there –
Fighting against despair –
Until the storm abated and their hope

Rose with the warming sun;
    Perhaps a boat would come
To end their hunger and thirst's painful scope.

    Then, like a dove in flight
    Hove a tall ship in sight,
Gliding towards them across the smooth wastes.
    Anxiously then, the three
    Waved to her frantically
Till she replied to them and they were saved.

    So they arrived one day
    Where a calm harbour lay
And were set down on that African shore
    Which had been their intent
    Before *Pelican* went,
With her brave crew, to the dim ocean-floor.

Future Hope

Ancestral country of my dearest kin
            I come,
Unprejudiced, with liberal intent;
        Peace I bear in my hands.
My heart aches at your misery and shock.
            My eyes
        Weep for your desolate despair.
        I sense your moidered hurt.

My death upon your bloodied land would bring
            Neither
Your factions' failure nor success to you –
        It would not signify –
Else would I gladly bleed. I am part you,
            For I
        Have sired five Anglo-Irishmen
            As my posterity.

Ancestral country of my dearest kin,
        Be still!.
Calm your fierce passions which stir so much grief
        And futile bitterness.
I pray for peacefulness to fill your heart
        Founded
        On reasoned tolerance and love.
        There lies your future hope!

Dragon

Snake-neck extended like an armoured lance;
    Croc-toothed flame-jaws agape; spike-tongue out-thrust;
      Black smoke-trails from broad nostrils streaming; barb-
      Tipped, saw-fretted writhe-tail all alash; huge
    As a whale: a Dragon is watching me
As closely as a tiger eyes potential prey!.

Now, with a potent surge of sudden force
    The great scaled monster, on membranous wings,
      Swoops down from its high cavern-den – like some
      Vast fiery eagle hastily astoop,
    Crook-claws flexed wide to grasp my cringing flesh –
Its bloodshot reptile-stare fixed balefully on me!.

Down through the windless air it quickly drops
    On half-furled, hook-fringed, whistling wings, intent
      On death. Merciless-eyed and furnace-mouthed
      It comes, talons extended for the strike!.
    With panic-pounding heart I wake to find
That Dragon a mere figment of my myth-fed mind!.

St. George

(23rd April)

    Lance couched you launched full at the giant foe;
The pestilential, flame-shot breath you braved;
The vicious talons, mighty tail, gross jaws
Contended; and triumphantly subdued:
Not for *your* glory but to liberate,
From monstrous tyranny, the innocent.
    Long years ago our Patron you became
And your Cross-emblem proudly we displayed
For centuries: whilst in more recent times
Your courage we adopted, as our own,
When greater evils stalked our continent
Laying it waste. Like you, we overcame.
    Forever, brave St. George, watch over England's parts
    And, in adversity, encourage English hearts!

Fourteen Eighty-Five – [I]

(Monday 22nd August 1485)

    This was the Year of the Red and the White.
Red blood and white flesh but the signs to tell
How Roses red and white had come to blow
In bloody conflict in bleak Redmoors marsh;
With red ambitions, white ideals involved
Red Dragon and White Boar in fatal feud.

    That was no quarrel between Wrong and Right,
But culmination of dynastic fate
Engendered thirty years before, when York
And Lancaster adopted, each their badge,
The White Rose and the Red to difference
Their proud supporters in controversy.
    Raw red ambitions marched together with
High white ideals of government and law

To bring brave heirs of partial families,
(Richard Plantagenet, the Yorkist king
And Henry Tudor, hopeful scion of
Lancastrian pretensions to the Crown),
To this rough place in armoured panoply
And all the plangent pomp of chivalry;
Together there, at England's central heart,
In Trial-by-Combat to decide, at last,
The mastery of England's fractious State.
    No clear-cut principle divided them,
That White Boar king and that Red Dragon earl;
Only shared dreams of power moved their minds
And brought them to this fateful field of war
Midway from Nottingham's and Leicester's walls.

    This was the Day of the Red and the White.
At early dawn the Red attack began;
White's counter-stroke not long delayed to join
Both causes in the business of death.
Crude cannon roared and whistle-arrows flew
In deadly cross-fire at those serried ranks;
Lance, mace and sword with axe, pike, halberd strove
To gain the Golden Trophy of the day.

    This was the Hour of the Red and the White.
Seeing the young Pretender isolate,
The King attempted one bold act of chance.
Attended by the bravest of his lords
The Boar sought Dragon in a sudden charge
Which, if successful, won the day for him.
    But, at this crucial moment, treachery –
Raw red and unprovoked – frustrated him,
When White Hart chose Red Dragon, *not* White Boar!.

    The gallant White King died heroically
Almost within his axe's striking-range
Of that Red Earl he sought to end the fray.
His White Boar ensign now with claret stained
As rich, red blood from pale, white flesh ran free;

The White Rose wilted as the red flood flowed
And Red Rose burgeoned on its fair-fleshed food.

    From underneath a rough bush, (was it Broom?),
The dinted crown was pulled – whence it was swept
From off the dying White King's helm – and placed,
By White Hart, on the Red King's youthful brow
In recognition of his victory.

    All that remained – an Act of State – to wed
The White King's niece; so White to Red conjoin
In Tudor Rose's symbol of surcease
From fratricidal feudal anarchy;
That England might achieve united peace
Under the Tudor Dynasty, begun
On Redmoors Plain, (now known as Bosworth Field),
In this, the Year of the Red and the White.

Fourteen Eighty-Five – [II]

(Richard's Squire's Tale)

    Yes, I *was* there on that cursed day
When noble Richard lost his crown
Those twenty long, sad years ago.
    I was his squire, you know; the one
Who bore his helmet and his arms
Whenever he would put them off,
From time to time, to talk to his
Advisors on the battlefield.
    I was a young lad then, of course:
Hardly escaped my teens, in fact;
But I had been with him before,
My peerless general and lord,
On his campaigns; so I was not
A stranger to the fields of war.

There was an early start that day,
As I remember it. The king
Arose at five o'clock. I closed
Him in his armour before six.
He had no breakfast, being far
Too tense, as usual, to eat
Upon the morning of a fight.
    At half-past-six, accompanied
By the Lords Norfolk, Surrey and
Northumberland, with several
More worthies, he surveyed the land
On which the day's events would turn.
(I went along, of course, to be
Of service to His Majesty
Should he have any need of it).
    With practised eye he quickly saw
What dispositions must be made
To gain advantage from the ground
And spoke his orders quietly.
To Lord Northumberland he gave
Scarcely a word; that sullen earl
Requested, and was given straight,
Charge of the Rear Guard and Reserve.
No more was said. I thought the king
Mistrusted him and wished that he
Should not be too close to his side
During the crucial time to come.
    This was confirmed when, in aside,
He said to Norfolk and his son:
"We shall not see *that* Lord today:
And for myself I am not sad,
For I have quite enough of cares
With both the Stanleys holding off
On either flank of us. I fear
That, if we do not early win
Advantage over Richmond, they
Will soon betray me, though I hold
Lord Strange for their security;

For they are well aware that I,
Despite the treason he disclosed,
Will not take *his* life to account
For *their* bad faith in me, their king.
    I therefore rest my trust in you;
And, if the chance present itself,
I shall take opportunity
In hand to rout the upstart Earl
Before the Stanley's intervene
Or sly Northumberland defect".
    (These words, or similar, he spoke
Within my presence as we gazed
Down to the plain where Oxford's flag
Defined the rebels' Vanguard-lines;
For noblemen pay scant regard
To what their body-servants hear).
    Duke Norfolk answered, I recall:
"Your Majesty may trust in me,
Though Hell itself should gape-mouth come,
To keep your honour bright. My son
And I will hold Earl Oxford tight
Until God shall accord to you
The victory; that England still
By your just laws will be well ruled
For many years to come. But, if
It should be otherwise, I would
Not wish to serve a lesser king:
Better to die for one's belief
Than live forever apostate!".
    The king's pale features flushed, as bright
Flashed his rare smile from careworn face.
The two shook hands, (with Surrey, too),
As Richard warmly promised them
That, if the victory were his,
Then they would quickly comprehend
The favour of a grateful king.

    After another look around
The disposed troops of either side –

Including Stanley's double-threat
Poised at the margins of the field
To North and South – he then affirmed
The tactics of the day to all
Attendant on his royal words:
Then to his tent returned to sup
A goblet of cool wine.
                              Sat there
At ease, and seeming unconcerned,
He ordered that the battle-crown
Upon his helmet should be set.
"My Liege!": (involuntarily
I spoke my worried thought in tones
Unfittingly intemperate):
"I pray you not to so disclose
Your royal person, by that sign,
To notice of your enemies!".
    He glared at me a moment, as
Down on my knees I fell in shame,
For publicly upbraiding him.
The nobles watched him, nervously;
His anger could be sudden, fierce!.
But then he smiled, and gently said,
To the amusement of his lords:
"Since when have *you* been Counsellor
To me?. Yet I well understand
That what you say is uttered from
The love you bear my personage.
Yet see!. Am I not blazoned with
The Royal Coat-of-Arms?. And will
My Standards not accompany
My every movement: not to say
These Gentlemen?. How then shall *that* –
That slender bauble – catch the eye
Of anyone who has not seen
Those *larger* emblems of my State?.
I thank you for your kindness, but
I have determined, since it *is*
For that gold trinket that this rash

Adventurer has come into
My peaceful realm to wage this war,
He shall have opportunity
To see it shine before his eyes,
Like mirages in deserts viewed;
And as untouchable by *him*!.
For I dare *any* man to try
To take it from me while I live;
He will not long survive my wrath!".
(He paused, his keen eyes sweeping round
The faces of attendant lords
Challengingly, before resuming).
"So, do not worry on this score.
Rather, beware of those whose faith
In our just cause is not secure;
For *there* my greatest danger lies!".
    (His words are graven on my heart:
As though with white-hot metal writ!.
Oh, noble monarch!. That his life
Was taken from us when it most
Promised such future happiness
For our land!. Oh, sad misfortune
When so great a heart as his, though
Contained within such little space,
Should be so wasted!. And for why?.
Because some Lords, who better knew
That Buckingham – vile spirit! – had
Destroyed those Royal Wards who stood
Between *him* and the crown he craved –
And for that wickedness had been
By slandered Richard put to death –
For their own partial vantages
Continued to perpetuate
That calumny against the king!.
Such petty reason for so foul
A deed as to betray their Liege!).

    Trumpets ring out as Norfolk sees
The rebel force advance towards

Our battle-lines beneath the flags
Denoting Oxford's leadership.
The king leaps up, excitedly,
To watch how matters will unfold.
    Commands are shouted. Scurriers
Rush back and forth between the bands
Of armoured companies. Loud guns
Explode their stone missiles amongst
Our serried ranks, and arrows sigh
Their litanies of death.
                                    (I still
Recall that sound with dread, even
After so many years!. It is
A noise more fearful than the blast
Of bombast cannon, which is much
More sound than great effect; unlike
Those yew-drawn barbs that, with less din,
Pierce armour-plate efficiently
At ninety paces with so straight
An aim as confounds foreign foes.
But I digress; the battle won't
Stand still for my parentheses!).

    The early fighting went our way
As noble Norfolk and his son
The gallant, loyal Surrey earl,
Honoured their promise to the king
By locking Oxford's van in grasp
Of iron weaponry. More than
An hour they battled handsomely.
    The king, meanwhile, observed all ways
The progress of the conflict and
The dispositions of the troops
Who held the struggle's outcome in
Hesitant hands and doubtful hearts.
From time to time he gave commands
For redeployment of reserves,
Sending some forwards to assist
Norfolk and Surrey in their skilled

Design to pin great Oxford down;
(For he was Richmond's general
Par excellence, experienced
And brave); so if he could be held
Until that moment when the king
Could act decisively, the day
Would end in victory for us.

    And suddenly that moment came!.
King Richard saw – what peerless gift
Of generalship! – that Richmond's group
Of personal retainers, (some
Twenty knights and noblemen), had
Moved out to the flank – determined,
As it seemed, to draw Lord Stanley's
Disengaged command to enter
The affray – and now was distanced
 From its Mainguard's defensive reach.
    "To horse!" cried Richard eagerly:
"Now let us shew this upstart earl –
Whose life was mostly spent abroad
In ignorance of our affairs –
How noble Englishmen can fight!".
    He took his helmet, crowned with gold
As he desired, from out my hands
But – as he went to put it on,
Giving a final glance around –
He saw the gallant Norfolk fall,
Leaving green Surrey in command
Against experienced Oxford's force.
    Yet Richard did not hesitate,
(Such wise war-leader as he was
Knowing this fleeting moment as
The battle's crucial turning-point),
A single instant. "Tell my Lord
Northumberland to move in aid
Of Surrey and assume control
Until I shall return!", he said,
(Hiding the doubts within his mind

Of that North lord's true loyalty);
Then put his helmet on and took
His heavy battle-axe in hand.
    Barons and knights prepared themselves
To fight. To my own horse I leaped;
My place beside my Sovereign
Wherever he might choose to go,
However hazardous it be.

    It must have made a splendid sight,
That last great charge of chivalry;
(I wish that I had witnessed it!
Hemmed in by others on all sides
I scarce could see in front of me
More than the rumps of horses, backs
Of men rigid in steel and clods
Of flying earth thrown up by hooves,
As down the slope of Ambion
Our battle-group descended),
Two hundred armoured knights, full-tilt
In blazoned surcoats rainbow-hued,
With banners flaring, weapons bright-
Gleaming in the sun; and silent!.
Silent, save the dreadful thunder
Of metalled destriers at speed!.
And at their head, astride his white
War-charger regally bedecked,
Rode Richard, last Plantagenet,
The bravest monarch of his line:
Its last and greatest warrior!.
    What noble scene we must have made
As nearer Richmond's bodyguard
We galloped down the sun-bright slope
Of Ambion's broad hill; down past
The inter-locked battalions
Of Surrey and Earl Oxford; down
History!. What fear did we rouse
In Richmond's heart as he looked up
To see us, like avenging Saints,

Descending on him?. Round him drew,
Protectively, his little band
Of knights attendant, as they set
Themselves to meet our closing force.

     The crash of contact was severe;
Riders to trampled earth were hurled
As maces stunned, sharp axes sheared,
Lances were shattered, sword-blades broke:
Death and destruction everywhere!.

     Then, at the very moment of
Anticipated victory,
Double-disaster came to us.
Stanley appeared upon our flank,
And with him twice a thousand men.
At that same instant Richard's horse,
Pierced with a pike, fell dead beneath
The king. What foul mischance was this?.
What fate?. One minute he was lost
Amid the wild confusion of
So many bodies, weapons, steeds
Thrashing the ground and air above.
Then he appeared again, his axe
Cleaving a swathe, a fighting-space,
About him as he made his way
Implacably towards his goal:
Richmond, Pretender to his Crown.
     I forced myself to him through press
Of flailing bodies, clashing steel
And raucous curses. "Here, my Liege,
A horse for you", I cried aloud,
"To save yourself!. Lord Stanley has
Betrayed you; all is lost!". The king –
Still single-minded in his aim,
Though hearing my impassioned cry –
Shouted full-voiced: "A horse?. A horse?.
My kingdom lost?. Not so!. I will
Dispose of this usurper yet!".

So he pursued his steadfast route,
Quite unsupported now, towards
His enemy. What slaughter then!.
I never saw a man fight so
Efficiently, destructively,
Until there stood before him none
Between him and the one he sought.
    Richmond would flee, but dared not so,
Else were the battle lost and all
His future hopes. He had to stay
And try defend himself against
This superhuman warrior,
The finest soldier in the world!.

    As Richard raised his dreadful axe
To save his realm, that very same
Time Stanley hurled his heavy mace.
It struck the king upon his helm,
Dislodging thence the crown. The king
Fell face to ground, but rose again
At once – armour for him was no
Impediment, he was so strong –
Determined to complete his plan
Though death should be the price he paid.
    A long lance pierced his iron back,
Another drove into his side;
Then dozens more assaulted him.
A further minute longer he
Stood there, defiantly, then cried,
(As from his nerveless hands, at last,
His lethal weapon fell): "Treason
Most foul has stole my crown away
From me!. Treason!. Treason!. Treason!".
And then he fell upon his back,
That he might still face his chief foe
Right to the instant of his death.

    (I saw all this amidst the fray
For, being a mere squire, I was

No worthy warrior for those
Seeking to claim a trophy-head
Or catch a ransomable lord.
So I was only twenty yards
Away, ignored by all; their eyes
Upon the drama of my king's
Demise at Richmond's very feet).

    So perished Richard, England's king,
Upon the Bosworth battlefield.
No other monarch ever ruled
So wisely as that noble man;
No other man had ever died
With courage so supremely great.
    His title may be lost; his life
May from his body be divorced
By violence and treachery;
But even his worst enemies
Daren't take away from him, at last,
The honourable way he fought
And died defending, on that day,
With courage, daring, pride and skill
His claim to England's governance.

    Yes, I *was* there on that cursed day;
And after all these years I still
Mourn for my Master and my King,
Whose words I heard; whose deeds I saw.
Nobody ever can compare
With his instinctive chivalry
Or with the largeness of his mind.
    So leave me, now, and let me grieve
In solitude again; until
Dear death my heart shall reunite
With him; the bravest of the brave
And last, great hero of our race!.

Fourteen Eighty-Five – [III]

(Henry's Squire's Tale)

You see this silver hair, these shaking hands,
In one aged forty?. Shall I tell you how
A man so young became so sudden-aged?.
   It was then; upon that famous day when
King Henry won his crown at Bosworth Field
Exactly twenty years ago. Before
That I was youthful, handsome, chestnut-haired
And skilled in all the arts of chivalry
Learned in the friendly lists of Tournaments
In France, exiled from England since my Lord
Claimed that the crown was rightly his to wear.
I was the body-squire and personal
Attendant of the King – who was mere Earl
Of Richmond at that time.

                     It was a day –
That of the battle of which you enquire –
So armour-bright and beautiful, it seemed
Great pity to have fighting as one's work.
   It all began quite early, if my mind
Recalls the details properly. At five
The noble Earl of Richmond roused himself
From sleepless bed. He ate a hearty meal:
"Men should not fight on empty stomachs, lad!",
Before commanding me to buckle him
Inside his battle-suit. (In age he was
Eight years my senior but yet aspired
To take the Throne of England, as his right,
By dispossessing from that lofty seat
The ill-reported monarch who had raised
Himself over the bodies of his Wards –
King Edward and his brother, minors both –
Of whom he was the regent-Governor.
   Richmond, himself next nearest to the Crown,
Was not content that England's king should be

Brought to that Honour by foul mischiefry.
For safety's sake, in France, he had prepared
With kin of those poor, murdered babes, his plans
To set aside the villain who then reigned
And, in himself, refurbish England's fame.
(But I digress!).

              Soon after breakfast came
A tense discussion with Earl Pembroke – who
Was Richmond's uncle – and Earl Oxford, most
Experienced war-leader on our side,
How best to manage that day's main events
Until the doubtful Stanleys intervened –
If intervene they would! – and on *whose* part?.
(Nobody there would wager very much
That *either* Stanley would participate
Until the issue was already clear!).
   Oxford would take the Van and keep it close,
Holding the larger force of Richard's power
And trying to commit such of its strength
As might expose a weakened place to which
The promised help of Stanley could be drawn
Before the king could win decisive sway
With his superior arms and generalship.
Lord Pembroke with Earl Henry would remain,
To counsel him at crises of the fight.
   "I fear me", Richmond said, "that this may be
A day of hardship for us all to bear.
Each man must do his best, and more indeed,
For victory to come. Would I were sure
Sly Stanley were for me: with Percy, proud
Lord of Northumberland, who hates the king!.
I spent the night in prayer – after return
Back from both Stanley camps – that Holy God
Would give us aid against this crooked king;
For, if God does not help, then we are lost!".
   "Now, Henry", answered Pembroke, "that's no way
To face a day so vital for our cause!.
Whatever private feelings you may have

You will not be alone in them, I know;
But you must put dissemblance on – a mask
Of confidence and bravery – that those
Who take your part today be not unmanned
By such contagious, melancholy thoughts.
Smile, then!. Be generous with hope!. And leave
To God decisions which *you* cannot make!".
    (A squire learns much that others don't, because
The high nobility assume he's safe
And just ignore his silent presence there).

    Richmond, impatient now of more delay
Which might bring further aid to England's king
Should vacillating Stanley so decide,
Told Oxford to prepare his men and then,
As soon as may be, set the battle on.
    That rough, brave man of war, Lord Oxford, laughed:
"Your Grace would like to take his midday meal
With England's golden crown upon his head?.
So be it, then!. But if, by some mischance,
It should turn out some other way, know this:
Better to try, but fail, than never make
Attempt to reach ambition's pinnacle!.
Today great glory, or obliquity,
Shall sit upon your brow. My soldier-hope;
That neither shall too dearly have been bought!.
Now, I into the Van, to set in train
The day's activities, and all our fates".
    Him gone, Lord Pembroke said: "Upon that Earl
We all do lay our lives; for he alone
Has the experience to win this fight.
Yet England has such leadership today,
Commanding numbers which we cannot match,
That even Oxford cannot overcome;
Unless those in the margins come our way
In time to succour us against this king.
But we must not dwell overlong on this,
Or hesitation will undo our cause!".

Soon trumpets shout; we all to horse at once,
As Oxford sets his troops in brave advance
And closes with Lord Norfolk's bold array.
The battle-lines engage; the struggle starts
Which will determine this momentous day.

Although at Tournaments I often watched,
This is my first experience of war:
And it is horrible!. So many deaths,
So many frightful injuries sustained
From arrow, sword and lance, from pike and mace
And scything battle-axe!.
       But, worst of all,
We see great Oxford slowly yielding ground
To skilful Norfolk's well-planned strategy,
As down the slope of Ambion he rolls
That armour-plated phalanx which he leads.
Lord Pembroke to Earl Oxford sends reserves,
(Led by Earl Talbot, then Lord Arundel),
Until there are left no more to commit
In his support; but Norfolk still gains ground!.

And then impatient Henry intervenes:
"I will to Stanley now, and bring him in
To join our cause, or kill the coward lord!".
He hotly speaks; nor does he heed Pembroke's
Cautious rebuke but angrily declares:
 "Uncle, it must be *now*, or we shall lose
This battle and its hoped-for consequence.
Another chance will never come our way,
For we must win or die this very day!"

Spurs to his charger's flanks he drove so hard
That blood appeared through gored caparison
As, like a quarrel from a crossbow flung,
Towards Lord Stanley's ranks he shot away!.
Some twenty Gentlemen-at-arms – with I
Myself amongst them, as my duty was –
Followed his hasty move towards the flank.

It was not long before we heard, above
The beat of hooves and fading battle-noise,
A sound like thunder overwhelming us!.
Raising our eyes, as round the Earl we reined
Our horses back, we saw descending from
The eminence of Ambion a host
Of riders, like a metal wall of death!.
How beautiful! – how terrible! – it was,
That tidal-wave of chivalry!. And there,
In front, on steed of foam, rode Richard, King
Of England; a great axe held on high, like
Some avenging Daemon sent from Hell's gates
To punish our brazen insurgency!.
    Fright froze us!. We would flee, but we could not.
We would speak, but words failed us. We would fall,
But armour held us stiffly in our seats!.
I felt the blood drain to my boots; my heart
Seemed stopped within my chest; cold sweat ran down
My face; time was suspended to my sense!.

    Oh God!. To die in such pathetic fear
Beneath the onset of that awesome horde!.
    Somehow a meagre front was formed in time –
What puny barrier to interpose
Between destruction and security! –
To shield our would-be-king from those who came
To castigate his impropriety
By taking of his hazard life itself.

    The shock of contact was intense; dying
Riders to trampled earth were hurled; flags fell;
Sword-blades shattered, lances broke; injury,
Death and destruction everywhere about:
Nowhere to go, nothing to do, but die
Selling our lives as dearly as we might!.

    Then, at the very nadir of despair,
A double-miracle appeared to us!.

Stanley himself arrived in the *melée*
Along with some two thousand men or more.
And at that self-same instant Richard fell,
His charger spitted on abandoned lance!.
"Thank God!", I shouted, as my tensions snapped,
Released from every pore of my shocked skin,
At this deliverance from certain death.

    It was not over yet!. King Richard rose
On foot, axe in his mail-gloved fist, keen eyes –
From opened face-guard – fixed where Richmond sat
Nearby, upon his horse, hemmed round with guards.
Though isolated now, cut off from help,
Surrounded by a hostile company
Who kept his own knights from assisting him,
King Richard quite disdained to cede the fight.
He took no thought for flight to save his life,
(Though someone offered him a horse for that),
But grimly battled nearer to the Earl
Who was the target of his obsessed heart.
    He thrashed his bloody path towards the spot
Where Henry, Earl of Richmond, sat as tranced.
No man could stand before that fierce attack
Spurred by the impetus of his will's aim.
Bodies fell right and left of him; bodies
In front fell, scythed down by his brutal strength,
Skilful technique, implacable resolve.
He seemed invincible as he advanced
Remorselessly towards the Earl, his goal;
Of warrior-kings a true *epitome*!.
    (Was this the monster, then, of whom I'd heard
So many stories?. Was this the evil
King who murdered babes?. Was this the tyrant
Hated by all men?. Somehow, within me,
Admiration rose above such fabled
Loathsomeness!).
            Alone, quite unsupported,
(So small in stature yet so great in heart!),
Still he pressed forward to his chosen prey –

My Liege-lord Richmond – loudly giving voice:
"Treason!. Treason!" many times; as well might
He cry, indeed, for he *had* been betrayed!.
Yet not one moment did he cease to wade
Through blood and bodies, swinging his dread axe
With marvellous efficiency – as once
 Harold at Hastings, to keep his kingdom
Or to die in the attempt, had assailed
Norman invaders – though, like him, in vain!.

    From out the throng behind him someone threw
A mace, which knocked him down. Again he rose;
Again he smote about him lustily,
Until some pikemen drove their weapons through
His undefended back and side. He fell
Face up, his eyes fixed on the Earl even
In death; and so, at length, King Richard died,
The last Plantagenet, on Bosworth Field.
His was a splendid death to make; the sort
That leaves you proud he was an Englishman!.
    (I've often wondered, since, how it could be
That such a brave and chivalrous demise
Could be with wicked reputation matched;
But there's no worth in speculation now).

    And so it was that Henry won the crown.
(I think they found it in a hawthorn-bush;
Though how it got *there* I will never know,
Who witnessed all these things with my own eyes!).
    But what I *do* know is, that I will not –
So long as my life lasts – forget the sight,
(So beautiful!: so terrible!), of that
Majestic charge of noble chivalry
Which almost lost, for us, the battlefield –
Which put a score of years upon my life,
Inflicted me with constant-quaking limbs
And prematurely turned my hair to grey –
Upon that day when Henry won the Crown
On Redmoors Plain near Bosworth's market-town.

Autumn Evening

The watercolours of an Autumn evening wash
    The sky, above the darkling Western hills, with stains
    Of intermingled pink, pale gold, green-violet.
Against this lambent backdrop stand the distant trees
    Poised in stark, uncompromising poses, more clear
    In outline, now, than at the hazy noonday's height.
Eastwards, the heavy heavens glower moodily
    Over the countryside whose detailed features fade,
    By imperceptible degrees, to nothingness.
Only the point-lights of some scattered stars relieve
    That superseding uniformity of dark,
    Drab daubs of overlying nebulosity.
Here, at the margins of both light and shade, I sit in awe
Of that great Artist who was, is and shall be, evermore.

In Good Time

This life of ours has much of grief and woe:
    How it will end we none of us do know;
    And that is just as well for us, since we
Have quite enough of present misery!.
We should not seek to learn too much too soon:
    In His good time we'll get God's promised boon
    Of perfect happiness; and then we'll know
Why this imperfect life has been made so!.

Seduction

Surely the charming phrase, the lavish gift,
    The brilliant display, are mere attires
    Of courting-rituals, designed for swift
        Submission to lust's transient desires?.
Do not the birds and beasts, to gratify
    Instinctive urges, flatter each their sort
    With such overt expressions, to comply
        In consummating ardour – then depart?
Seduction has one target for its art
    Which, once achieved, extinguishes the flame
    That warmed its passion, leaving a hurt heart
        Abandoned by indifference to pain.
So is this what you want from me?. Or would you have
The subtler secrecies of more enduring love?.

In Your Experience

(for Heidi)

Knowing that you've delivered life,
    After nine months' creative wait,
Should be conceived love incarnate
        In your experience.

Feeling your baby nuzzle close
    Within your arms towards your breast
Should be, amongst life's joys, the best
        In your experience.

Sensing that from yourself there flow
    Health-giving streams of nourishment
Should be a source of deep content
        In your experience.

Sharing those incidents that teach
    Life's lessons to a growing mind
Should be an education twined
    In your experience.

Seeing your cherished child achieve
    Maturity's wise adulthood
Should be the end of parenthood
    In your experience.

Holiday

    A few short hours of homeliness –
Snatched minutes of sheer bliss –
Before returning to the drudge
Of working under constant stress.
How we love each carefree moment
Of release before we trudge,
Back to our obliged employment!.
    Yet, it is their very briefness
That give holidays their charm;
Too much time squandered remiss
Could provoke us to some harm,
Or quickly lose prized preciousness.
A short while passed with those we hold most dear
Brings more enjoyment than an idle year.

Pain

    I've a pain in my heart,
But I do not know if
    Its ache is a part
Of my death or my life.

Is it pain which denotes
That my heart is diseased?
    Or a pain which reports
My emotions' unease?.

Is it psychosomatic
    Or physical pain?
Is it just emblematic
    Or meaningful bane?

Doubtful although its meaning be
My pain is not less real, for me!.

Nature's Gossips

Along the margins of some forest paths
Fresh, purling rivulets run noisily.
  They are wild Nature's gossips and will tell
    The seasons of the year in tones that brook
  No arguments from sceptic minds. They'll say
Where foxes' dens and badgers' setts are hid;
  Where shy deer browse beneath low boughs, hares box
Or rabbits burrow. If you wish, they will
  Retail where thrush and blackbird nest; or where
    The nightingale sings softly, deep in shade;
    What place the spiral skylark briefly puts
  Its fragile foot to ground; where night-owls haunt.
Such gossiping I never heard, before my home
Was in *Coolmela* and my senses free to roam.

Xanthippe

When he could speak, the mild philosopher observed:
  "You seem to take much pleasure telling me, forever,
    My faults and foibles. I have never claimed to be
A flawless paragon; not even in those days –
  So *long* ago they seem! – when we were courting lovers
  And I thought *you* personified perfection: dared
To tell you so. (No doubt that was an error, too!).
  Since I am so much in the wrong, (if not alone
    In that), isn't there still *some* failing known to you
Which has not *yet* been mentioned?.
                        But enough of moan
  And groan. Listen: I'm doing my best to deliver
  You *your* vision of myself; though it's not my *own*!.
Now, I've important work to do which must not be deferred;
So let me have a little peace. And don't be so *absurd*!.

Reason and Imagination

(Non Sequitur?)

  I like sound reason. (Just imagine it!).
Cool logic, commonsense and practical
Utility, dealing in factual
Objective *phenomena*!.
                Ag'in' it
Set subjective, anarchistic feeling
Leaping from lairs in dark subconsciousness,
(Where untamed instincts prowl a wilderness
Of chaos), radically revealing,
Unpredictable.
              Imagination's
Effects unsettle the calm intellect
With irresponsibility, respect
Only vague noumenal intimations.

Yet reason wreaks more havoc, in life's troubled course,
Than wild imagination's raw, primæval force.

.

Poetry and Bathostry

Poetry and Bathostry are antitheses.
That is momentous, descriptive, evocative,
Memorable perfection, controlled and gracious thought,
Which draws a comprehensible picture of life
In metrical designs of vivid artistry.
Shapeless, undisciplined, prosaic, vague, *This* is
Arhythmic, ungrammatical and trivial,
Unpolished, unimaginative, dull,
Unlovely, colourless; a travesty of *That*.
If *This* is Bathostry – the rife disease of change
Infecting countless minds with its infirmity –
Whose victims heedlessly reject those principles,
(On grounds of age alone), which have enriched the world
Through time with genius – then *That* is Poetry.

Erineceus.

Secretive
Echinoderm –
Pulex-porter –
Oviraptor –
Hail-ward –
Anti-alopecian –
Wood-urchin –

Nocturnal earth-miner –
    Sea-less mine –
        Gastronome
Of *gastropoda*,
    Insecta, cadavera –
Sun-symbol fire-friend –
Armed hero of peace –
    Inoffensive sword-ball –
Fierce *ophidia*-fighter –
Contractile contradiction –
        Hedgehog.

[**N.B**. These are all epithets for the hedgehog, gathered from ancient Greek and numerous subsequent sources].

Lochmatt

(for Ingrid)

I've travelled through so many lands
  And stayed in splendid places,
Yet rarely have I ever found
  A residence whose graces –
Warm welcome, simple comforts
  And *environs* sublime –
Have tempted me to linger
  Beyond contracted time.
But *Lochmatt* was such pleasure
  That I was loath to leave;
So when I next have leisure
  I hope you will receive
Beneath its roof, as grateful guest,
One who appreciates the best.

Lyric Skylark

Often I've stood on some wide upland swell
And heard a lyric skylark, higher still,
Spiral abroad its fantastic refrains
Of liquid descants as it poured pure notes
Into the whorls of my astounded ears.
Surging aloft on pulsing wings, it trilled
With all the burbling fervour of its heart
In joyous roundelays which brightly whirled
Into my captivated consciousness.
If I had half that small bird's happiness,
Then I might always be enraptured; but,
Being mere mortal, I cannot aspire
To joys angelical. When I must die, I'll be
Content to hear its soaring sky-song welcome me.

Music and Poetry

(A 'Neapolitan' Poem)

Rich streams of suasive sound arouse in open hearts
Emotions which can overmaster reasoned thoughts.
Skilled music stirs our minds with flowing tides
Which wash our senses' and our souls' insides.
Rare poetry inspires our minds to reach
For excellences nothing else can teach.
As clinging folds of cadence wrap our sense,
Like Summer pines, in pleasant redolence,
Associations of the deepest kind
In myriad diversities we find;
Even wire-throated violins may sing
Their hair-wrung songs and rosined passions wring;
Whilst powerful, apt words intoxicate

Our raptured thoughts and our emotions sate,
As crafted orchestrations adumbrate
Visions of angel-harmonies more great.
Effulgent magnaminities of sound
Induce inceptive dreams of hopes unbound;
Whilst fluent notes, dissolving as they rise,
Dispel tight tensions and disharmonies.
The glory of one perfect phrase, word, tone
May be compared to any treasure known.
Evocative intricacies of sound ignite
Profound emotions that can set our souls alight.

[A 'Neapolitan' is a poem in which alternate couplets, or other groups of lines, refer to contrasted things – in this case poetry and music – and thus combines two or more separate poems into a third. The name is derived from the cake, or ice-cream, in which layers of different colours, tastes or other ingredients are superimposed.]

Larksong in War

Hear how expressively small skylarks wring
From shell-shocked throats incendiary songs
Which burn into crushed consciences the pains
Of conflict and its needless suffering.
Self-mortaring into smoked skies, the larks
Explode in tonic shrapnels which pierce through
Hate-deafened ears to lodge, deep in hurt hearts,
Hot fragments of sharp ecstasy which tear
Smashed spirits past description of worn words.
But such exquisite injuries can cure,
Not kill, war-wounded sensibilities,
(As skilful surgeons' scalpels heal what swords
Have hewn or shells have shattered senselessly),
Through their reviving art's felicity.

Time and Art

"Since they both are things apart,
　　What has Time to do with Art?",
　　　　Is the sceptic's scornful cry.
"Art emerges from Time's heart,
　　So they can't be things apart",
　　　　Is the poet's prompt reply.

Xanadu

(History and Myth)

Xanadu, exotic name,
Drawing its hypnotic fame
　　From a Coleridge dream-shot fit,
(Stirred by Polo's rare report
Of rich Kublai Khan's resort),
　　Through a drug-induced remit.

Xanadu – or Great X'ian –
Was the place where first began
　　China's Empire under Shi:
There his terracotta Horde
Still keeps guard about its Lord
　　In his posthumous degree.

Xanadu stood near the Wall –
Largest artefact of all
　　Human ingenuity –
Fifteen hundred miles in length
To intimidate the strength
　　Of prospective enemies.

Many centuries have blown
Since those ramparts of dressed stone,
    (And that terracotta Force),
Were deployed to help police
Shi's new Middle Kingdom's peace
    And sustain his Empire's laws.

Polo saw these sights himself
As he traded Kublai's wealth:
    Coleridge dreamt them into myth.
Kingdoms rise and Empire's fall,
Yet that Army and this Wall
    Scowl on, fierce as Dragonsteeth.

Powerfully redolent
Of huge might, (but impotent
    In the land they should defend),
Still they stand, mute symbols now
Of ambitious dreams, and how
    History and Myth contend.

Shi's hid Funerary Hall
One day will reveal to all
    Wonders to astound the view:
History and Myth shall then
Be compatible again
    There, at famous Xanadu.

<u>Composition</u>

(from: *A Theory for Art*, xix)

When I compose my poetry I sense,
Within myself, a feeling of unrest:
A quiet, self-sustaining turbulence…
    Control of what I think and write becomes
A *shared* experience – another brain

Seems to be integrated with my own
And offers me the rough ingredients
I need!. It helps me to manipulate
Thoughts into comprehensible designs.
    And all the while I hear the pulsing notes
Of music harmonising with my moods,
Assisting me form waves of words which pour,
(Like raging cataracts or waterfalls),
Onto the page beneath my pencil-point.
Symphonic scores or operatic airs
Suffuse my working minds, (or else a flood
Of lyric songs or ballad-tunes, awash
With my invention's own *motifs*), to match
The stream of composition. (I regret,
Now, that I did not persevere with my
Youthful attraction to musical modes
Since – had I *then* learned knowledge how to write
My thoughts upon the staves – *now* might the tones
Of melic, stimulating chords be heard
Along the air-waves of the Earth, to clothe
A fresh dimension on my poet's voice,
And not be lost to fading memory).
    For poetry is music, to my sense,
And verse which does not own some musical
Effect is scarcely poetry, for me.

Poetry and Music

    "If music and sweet poetry agree
As they must needs, the sister and the brother",
Then in our poems music should be found,
And in our music should be poetry.
    The one is inextricably enwound
Within the very being of the other,
And to divide them is to take from each
Some quintessential aspect of its nature;
So rendering defective by that breach
The finest quality of its best feature.

That's not pure music which lacks in each phrase
The influence of true poetic sense;
Nor's that great poetry which gives offence
By reason of its want of music's grace.

Sunlit Waterfalls

"Here lies one whose name was writ in water".

[*Epitaph*: tomb of John Keats at Rome].

Though water seems an unsubstantial thing
Having no shape that may be called its own,
(Unlike some monument of carven stone),
It is, in nature, mightiest: the king
Of forces which determine life and form.
So he who claimed his name was writ therein
Spoke truer than he thought!. There has not been
Another poet, since his time, whose charm
Could open magic casements in the souls
Of those who love pure beauty, or delight
In memorable lines. His words run bright
Down through the years, like sunlit waterfalls
Whose rainbowed spectacles enthral all those who see
The ageless splendours of their moving majesty.

Natural Memories

i.
Too often, in my life, I found myself
Exiled from England –
Country of my birth
And great sustainer of my dreams;

Home of my culture
And rare cricket's poetry –
And recollected, in my loneliness,
Those absent beauties which had pleasured me
Throughout my childhood
And long, youthful years
Spent deep in Suffolk
And in Somerset.
Sometimes, alien prospects stirred in me
A yearning for the lovelinesses known
Amongst green pastures and well-wooded slopes
Imprinted on my mind
When consciousness was still subliminal,
(And therefore most effective),
In the memories it learned:
And also scenes from later years, recalled
When more maturity informed my views
With broad significances of these things
Which had eluded callow interest.
Then I would see, upon my inner eye,
The vivid images that once I knew,
As clear as though they yet surrounded me
And not mere souvenirs of what had been.
Then I would hear, within my inner ear,
Those sounds which had enraptured me; as though
Dear dreamy scenes had come to life again,
Or had been captured on a mental film
Which now replayed them for my benefit
As solace in my exiled circumstance.
And I both see and hear them now
As I recall those absent years
And how I felt outside
My native country's island shores –
(On sweat-steamed, shadeless days when humid heat,
A sodden, heavy blanket, pressed me close,
Starting warm perspiration-rivulets
To flow in enervating streams across
Hot-pulsing skin; uncomfortable, fierce
And unrefreshing days of unrelief;

Or in the bitter chill of wintertime
In continental Europe, when the cold
Bit through my bloodless flesh with icy teeth
And gnawed my frozen bones until they ached –
                Still dreaming daydreams
            As I filtered through my mind
My life's experience, its hopes and fears,
            Still seeking to distil, somehow,
The essences of perfect happiness
                And that fulfilled
            Contentment rarely known.

                ii.
        My fondest recollections centre most
Upon the creatures which inhabited
The close woods, fields and hedgerows of the land
Which hid me in its hollows secretly;
Or boldly lifted me up high upon
                Its rolling hill-crests
            And steep-sided cliffs
Whence I could oversee the neighbourhood
Or stare across the restless ocean-waves,
Or merely gain perspective of myself –
            Within the broad context
                Of Nature's wild lone –
Whilst I sought peace in solitariness
As far from humankind as I could go,
Where untamed shaggy ponies on bleak moors
Steam-breathed from nostrils flared at chilly dawns,
Or placid cattle-herds meandered slow
            Across wide fields, contentedly
Or, in more narrow country lanes,
                Congestedly;
And sheep, like stones, were scattered far and near,
White outcrops in an all-pervading green;
And massive saddlebacks – whose rotund bulk
            Belied remarkable agility –
Rooted amongst the hedges and the trees
            For succulent delicacies

Buried amid
The *débris* of the year;
Or in the Lowland Borders and the high
Bare bens of Scotland, where I saw
Stout, matt-haired, wide-horned Highland cattle roam
Braving inclemency
With stubborn, stoic disregard;
Whilst, overhead, the cruciform
Great eagles wheeled, silently observant
Of every movement underneath their flight.
For, in the countryside,
Although alone,
You never *are* alone;
Sharp ears hear well your every step,
Keen eyes observe each move;
The country-creatures curiously mark
Your actions and,
(If you don't offer threat),
They come to share your company awhile
With unselfconscious,
Innocent delight.
At such chance meetings I could soon forget
The cares and tribulations of my life
In calm acceptance of these creatures' natural
Spontaneous activities.

iii.
My mind recalls them
With affection now, no less
Than when I first encountered them and thrilled
With wonder at their beauty and their grace,
My eyes and ears absorbing each nuance
Of unpremeditated artlessness.

For I have seen
Expansive fields in which,
Stirred by the tidal-motions of the wind,
Tall grasses ebbed and flowed as though
They formed the surface of some hedge-locked sea;

And other fields,
Like star-lit green Heavens,
Dark starling-spangled
In the evening glow
And sonorous
With whistling, whirring life.

And I have seen
So many quiet cemeteries where
The berried yew
Still shades the buried youth
Of wars beyond our disremembering.

And I have seen
Green florets on fir-branches brightly glow
With televisual intensity
Against dawns' growing light
And hillside pines
Blush copper-trunked at rising of the sun,
Or rust as though decayed
In fading sunsets.

And I have seen
Huge flocks of starlings, intermixed
With pigeons, rooks and 'pies,
Thicken the air above my head
And darkly cloud the skies:
The while my senses were transfixed
To hear their mingled cries
And see their perturbations spread
Abroad before my eyes.

And I have caught
Glimpses of stealthy mink
Escaped from barred captivity to roam
The wooded margins of the countryside.

And I have seen,
(Where waterlily pads

Float placidly upon the face
Of rivers, lakes, canals
Which are their natural moist habitat),
Milky swans – sail-wings unfurled –
Glide effortlessly on their way
Amongst tall, spikuled thistle-plants
Globe-crowned with regal, purple diadems.

And I have seen
On coasts he raucous gulls
Flock waves and beaches like ice-floes or foam
Whitening the waters
Or, on inland rubbish dumps,
Fighting for *detritus*-scraps as if
Their own survival were at stake.

And I have watched
Wild geese fletch noisily
Athwart autumnal skies
In the grey gloams of sullen dawns and dusks.

And I have seen,
On warmer days the handsome bullfinch,
Like a jewel, shine
Along the hedgerows of lone country lanes;
Their shades of pink, blue-grey, black, white,
Putting to shame
The very blossoms where they played;
And honey-hued
Squat yellowhammers flit
Like bloated golden bees amongst the sprays;
And pastel-plumed
Chirpy, quick chaffinches
Hop through dark hedges like magic, mobile,
Multi-tinted flowerlets, (pink and blue in brown,
Corporal-striped, pert-pointed pinions),
By brisk winds helter-skelter blown;
And hover-hawks
Hung Christ-like in the sky,

Borne on their unseen Crosses
        Of airy atmosphere.

        And I have seen
    And heard the pale-eyed, sooty jackdaw
        With its mimic tongue,
    And the crested, blue-patched jay,
    Together with their cousin magpie
        In its bright bi-toned livery;
A sharp-eyed, bold triumvirate who form
        A robber-gang of deft alacrity
            Whose members steal
        All glitter-objects they espy
    To dress their nests and complement
        Their noisy, feathered vanities:
            True popinjays!.

        And I have seen,
    (Where reds and golds, all flecked
With yellows, browns and varied shades of green
    Sear a rare grandeur on the dying year),
        Shy deer lift watchful heads
            Amongst the leaves
    To stare in ruminative calm,
    (The while their supple muscles tensed
    For instant flight instinctively),
        Before resuming their
Browsing of the foliage, untroubled
By my openly unthreatening approach.

                iv.
        And I have smelled
    The clinging, oily redolence
    Of clammy, tangy damp pines;
Rare floral fragrances inhaled;
And breathed the odours which arose
When morning mists from sheltered lakes
    Ascended to the brightening skies
        Between the steaming trees,

As though there burned, beneath
   The opaque interface
   Where water melts to air,
The smoking campfires of a mighty host
   Concealed from my occluded sight.

v.
And I have heard
   The skies creaking with crows,
      Thick-massed on ragged wings,
         Beating Autumnal dusks;
And from beneath my careful feet –
Near where the timid fieldmouse and the small,
Shy vole conceal themselves beneath
         The tangled undergrowth –
The sudden, loud-winged pheasant leap,
Shouting a startled '*Cok-cok, cuk*'
In high-pitched resonances raised
Above the whirring clamour of its swift
         Departure from that hiding place.

And I have heard,
   In shaded woodland-deeps,
      The unseen pulsing throbs
         Of night-hid wings
In frightened flutters from the dark leaves stir;
      And hedges rattle
   With unruly magpie throngs;
      And sombre coaltits in
      Their sober plumage '*wheep*'
Amongst the berried branches,
      Mournfully discreet;
         And blackbirds
With their orange-yellow bills,
(Like golden whistles with black ribbons tied),
Outpouring through those shining instruments
      Pure music's liquid modulations:
         More magical than human arts
            Have ever conjured yet.

I have known
The haunting howl of the hunting owl
Pierce my pale consciousness with dread
Beneath the dead-eyed moon; and heard
The brown-beaked bittern boom
Where rusted reeds stood ranged in ranks
Along the slow canals' slight banks;
And vixens scream
In depths of night
Whilst foraging for food for cubs
Whose shrill voracity demands more meat;
And the clattering cries
Of the loud magpies
Shatter those silences where
Bright, swift, snake-water-runnels slide
Their shining scales through forest paths
After a sudden shower.

vi.
Sometimes, rarely,
I have seen the hoopoe
In its pale pink plumes, with crested crown
Aflutter in the breeze, spread barred wings wide
To catch the Summer sun.

And I have seen
Broad hillsides where
The massive shirehorse hauls the heavy plough
To open up the fertile soil
In preparation for its future crops.

And I have seen
The dainty, russet fox
(Where sempiternal gorse-blooms burn
In valley, field and hedge, on rock and hill),
Picking its careful way –
Ears pricked, sharp nose to ground,
Keen eyes alert – tracking its prey;

Whilst countless rabbits gambolled in play,
White scuts a-bob, beside their warrens
          Near thick bramble-shrubs,
          Seeming oblivious
     Of that sly predator's approach, until
The look-out's sudden stamp despatched
Them to their burrows in a rush
Of flurried furry legs and laid-back ears.

          And I have seen
Huge hares chasing through the dewshot leas
     In unconcerned lithe friskiness,
          Self-confident in their ability
     To outrun any danger save
The human hunter's lethal gun.

          And I have seen
     The thick-set badger at its sett
Or waddling purposefully on its trails
Along the margins of the woods and fields,
Long striped head swinging like a metronome
          In time with pacing paws.

          And I have seen,
     Amidst the marshes of East Anglia,
     The foreign coypus wading through
Thin weed-choked ditches as they chewed their way
     Towards the deeper, broader fenland dykes;
          And lean, slick otters gliding through
     Clear streams, or slipping up and down
          The banks like furry, playful giant eels;
And swift stoats sprinting through short grass
In bounding runs of svelt ferocity.

          And I have seen
     Tree-squirrels, red and grey alike,
          Display astonishing agility
Upon high branches, or bounce
Like animated furry balls

Across the open spaces between trees,
Flaring their tails like streams of smoke,
Whilst keeping watchful eyes aloft
Where pendant hawks patrol the air
Hunting for careless prey.

And I have seen
The blue-green-russet kingfisher
Burn bright in darting forays over ponds and streams;
And slow, grey, silent herons hunch themselves
In patient poses amid marshy wastes
Until their appetites have been assuaged.
The brash robin, unafraid to shew itself,
Has caught my eye –
The minuscule wren, too, despite its discrete ways –
By reason of their Winter fortitude
Which seems to well-epitomise
The providential grace
Of natural law.

vii.
These things, and many others, I have seen
And heard during my solitary walks
Beneath the crumpled clouds
Which lay like fallen curtains
Across the hilltops, smothering those heights
With moistly involute opacities –
And under open, sun-bright skies which lent
Added enchantment to experience –
Throughout my youthful years
'In England's green and pleasant land'.
These were the sights and sounds which most
Beguiled my exiled days and nights.
They brought to me
A peace and happiness I else had not achieved;
And they determined me to make return,
As soon as opportunity allowed,
To reacquaint myself with them once more
When I set foot again on England's distant shore.

And still these pleasures cancel exile's pain
As I remain
Unable to surround myself
With the realities
Which have engendered these
Natural memories.

The Death of Harold

(14 October 1066)

Outnumbered, but undaunted, stood the English king
Near Hastings, with his close-embattled shield-wall-ring
And steadfast axemen, beating off incessantly
Renewed assaults of Normandy's horsed chivalry.
Late was the hour, and soon would darkness bring
reserves
To join his battered ranks and freshen wearied nerves.
With hopes thus reinforced, England could yet be saved
When these hard-fought hostilities were next rebraved.
Why, then, did he look up?. His brain – with colours
starred,
With blinding lights and agonising pains – was scarred.
Backwards he staggered, clutching at the fatal fluke
Projecting from his peerless eye in sharp rebuke
To thoughts of glory!. Then he died; and his untimely death
Extinguished England's darkling hopes with his expiring
breath.

Illusions?

Some nights, from out the dark, I seem to see
Dim flicker-lights of stars behind thin mists
Which veil them to my focussed sight. Is this because
I think they're there, and so permit my brain
To turn my thought into apparent fact?.
Or is peripheral night-vision more acute?.
For, when I stare straight where those glimmers were –
all's blank!.
It's rather like those minds that search for God.
Some think He's there, and so they seem to see
His works made manifest about them; but when they
Look hard for something definite, by which
They can confirm His interest in them,
He vanishes completely from their view; as though
He never did exist – or else preferred to hide!.

Xiphos

Once, over Damocles, it swung
Suspended from a slender hair
And threatened him with sudden death.
Now, over our democracies,
The fatal sword of tyranny
Is poised to strike.
We should not sit
Inert, dismayed, like Damocles;
For our oppressive terror is
Chaotic anarchy itself,
Held in suspension only by
The fragile thread of decency;
And if we lose our nerve, we die.
Therefore, summoning courage, we should seize
The dread blade's hilt and disarm our unease.

Proportionality

(In flagrante delicto)

Tie them up – so! –
As Leonardo
Posed his 'Proportionate Man':
That at my leisure
I may then pleasure
My retributory plan.

Strip off their clothes
To starkly expose
Intimate attributions,
So each one can see,
With close clarity,
The sites of their collusions.

Fasten those chains
So their promised pains
Will not permit them relief;
For they must repay,
This very same day,
The debt they owe to my grief.

When you've done all,
Depart till I call
You to unloosen their chains;
To what else you hear
Just turn a deaf ear:
Punishment often brings pains!.

* * * * *

Now we're alone –
We three on our own –
Closed in this dungeon of tort,
You'll both feel and see
The sharp agony
Engendered by wanton sport.

    You dared ignore
  The threat which I swore
Should you give way to desire.
  Now you'll discover
    That this thwart lover
Burns with a violent fire!.

    You will regret –
  But never forget,
 Once you have felt my revenge! –
  Your impudent lust
    That cuckolded trust:
Dishonour I must avenge!.

    I will not shirk
  My pain-driven work
To chastise your carnal vice,
  Until you have met
    The ransom I've set
As immorality's price.

    Nor shall I haste
  To scourge your flesh chaste;
Pity is not in my thought!.
  You'll suffer so much ,
    As devices touch,
Where you'll wish they were not brought..

    The bitter whip
  Your stressed skins will rip,
And other instruments prise
  Those delicate parts
    Which led your lewd hearts
To gross infidelities.

    Never again
  Will freedom from pain
Lighten your lives' misery:

My anger shall blight
    Each day and each night:
You'll wish you hadn't wronged me!.

* * * * *

    Now we're alone –
    We three on our own –
Here in my dungeon of dole,
    Should he – or she – first
    Endure the pains nursed
In the deep depths of my soul?.

[*Note*: Although Leonardo da Vinci's early-16th century AD *Notebooks* made the *'Proportionate Man'* image famous – it shews a naked man, spread-eagled like a star within a circle, as if tied to a frame – it was actually designed by the 1st century AD Roman architect Marcus Vitruvius Pollio to demonstrate the Principle of Proportionality, so it is sometimes called *'Vitruvian Man'*. I used Leonardo's name in my poem because he is far better known than Vitruvius.]

Venus-Plants

i.
(*Dionaea Muscipula*)

    A Venus-flytrap is a vampire-plant –
A carnivore – designed so cunningly
It seems as innocently generous
In free, luxuriant profligacy
As any nectar-yielding source could be.
    How openly it offers-up itself;
Its leaves – spread broadly bare and welcoming –
Mellifluous, exuding *ichor*, (sweet
To taste and censing pleasant *pheromones*),

79

Attractive to small insects foraging
In search of something ripe to drink or eat.
    Arriving at a leaf, each insect sups
The moist intoxicant contentedly,
(Like some debauchee deeply in his cups,
Oblivious of environmental space),
Until it touches, inadvertently,
One of the bristles scattered randomly
About the surface of that drinking-place.
    At once the sugared source snaps firmly shut,
Imprisoning the victim in a trap
From which there's no escaping certain doom,
Although it struggle to the last behind
The spine-barred window of that living tomb.
    From each small death the Venus-plant sucks life
For its own benefit; consuming flesh
To resupply itself with nutrients.
    Then sometimes, (strange as any miracle),
Appears a lovely blossom – delicate
And faintly smelling of rare-perfumed scents –
Which flourishes a brief while, then expels
Minute seed-spores to propagate afresh
Its ancient *species* in unchanging state.

ii.

(*Homo Sapiens Poeticus*)

    Don't poets, like the Venus-plant, adopt
Such subtle dispositions?.
                        Honeyed words
Attract the fascinated interest
Of minds in search of sensory rewards;
Their mellow phrases inundate held hearts,
Drown inhibitions and intoxicate
Profound absorption into disregard
For all except the pleasures they donate
In seeming liberality.
                        But those
Unfortunates who find themselves seduced

80

And overwhelmed by such devised delights
Of variegated verbal artistry
Into abandoned ecstasies, soon find
Themselves ensnared, unable to break free.
They squander their concerns on these induced
Desires – to satisfy their need for more
A*mbrosia* which, like *morphia*, now binds
Them in addictive thrall.
                         Those poet-minds
That first attracted them towards their source
Now feed upon their captives' inner selves
Voraciously.
            Unable to escape
Such all-consuming, self-sustaining force –
Predaceous, vampiric, vicarious –
Their victims are abstracted out of sense.
  Sensivore poets, absorbing the strength
Derived from such inalienable ties,
Put out fresh blossoms of rare poetry
That, in their potency, engender seeds
To guarantee the continuity
Of their own ancient *species* – which still breeds
Unchanged, as it has done through history –
Gaining their nourishment from others' needs.

I pose this parallel because I seem to see
(In plants and poets both), Blake's 'fearful symmetry'.

Under the Ice

Reputedly, Antarctica is rich in oils
  And minerals of every kind; sufficient spoils
    To whet our appetites in raw materials
      For industries. Constantly rise political
Disputes over the ownership of such rare store
  Under its miles-deep, age-protected ceiling-floor.

Yet, far more precious than these minerals are those
Fresh relics of pre-history which could expose
Immute forms for discovery; life's stages curbed
As frozen fossils – by humankind undisturbed
Since first they were laid down – our hidden future-past.
We must preserve these if we search for unsurpassed
New knowledge of old life and its advance by land and sea;
To prove, beyond a doubt, our long-contended ancestry.

Beyond Time's Spiral Wall

As far as Hubble's sharp, unblinking eyes can see –
Through plasmic time and space towards eternity –
Unending crowds of stars and galaxies appear,
(With their attendant cloudy *nebulæ*), as clear
As if they had ignited in quite recent days;
Yet at such distances as predicate their blaze
Must be more ancient than reason's best estimate.
Their complex natures confound theorists who state
The cosmic age has limits which can be divined
Through mathematic *formulæ* cast in the mind
By logic's clever arts.
Hubble, it seems, makes plain
The universe forever trades in loss and gain:
Recycling, in its changeful constancy, the fate of all
That was or is, to some new state beyond Time's spiral wall.

Naked Thoughts

Nakedly I go to bed
Every solitary night
To experience sensations
(Which my drowsing, dream-shot head
Films for me in imaged light),

Of that past day's situations
And their vivid evocations.

   Barely are my limbs composed
   In the comfort of their rest
Unconfined by inhibitions,
   Thoughts and concepts are exposed
   Which my conscious mind suppressed
Lest their flagrant exhibitions
Should transgress taste's prohibitions.

   Stripped of those obfuscing veils
   That concealed their privities
From perception's observation,
   They reveal their starker tales
   To appreciative eyes,
For æsthetic contemplation
And acute evaluation.

   Shorn of crude excrescences,
   (Which disfigure beauty's *ch'i*
By their ugly dispositions),
   They display, for my senses –
   In their artless artistry –
Their essential compositions
And implicit contradictions.

   Secret truths and beauties cause
   Inspirations to arise,
(Through sympathetic syntheses
   Of imagination's force
   And cognition's cultured eyes),
As freed cerebral faculties
Loose sensual capacities.

   Boldly, baldly in the sight
   Of my contemplating *ens*
Every exquisite perception –
   And each defect which can blight

Honesty's rare innocence –
Unadorned for my inspection
Naturally draws attention.

Raw experiences yield
Their materials as foods
For æsthetic transformations
Into concepts which can build,
Transcendentally, to moods
That, by their transfigurations
Can create such transmutations

As their consequential forms
Far surpass those mundane parts
That comprised their bare beginnings.
Now, shorn of strict social norms,
(Stripped of drossed, occlusive arts
Which disguise intended meanings),
They unveil truth's underpinnings.

Unconstrained, I analyse –
Through subconscious processes
Of discreet discriminations –
Qualities my inward eyes
Intimate each possesses
In the way of its relations
To perpetual revelations.

When these actions are complete
And evaluations done
To my private satisfaction,
Then my weary mind, (replete
With the pleasures it has won
From such fruitful rarefaction),
Sleeps in peaceful stupefaction.

Nakedly I go to bed
Every solitary night,
(With my drowsing brain divested

Of censorious 'blue lead'),
To review in sheer delight
Images surreally fed,
Like film-projections, through my head.

Winter Bridal

This slim, hoar-frosted Beech, in lacy traceries so bright
Now proudly stands, a stiff-silked Bride, upon her Wedding
Day
Behind her pose the darkly-congregated Pines, arranged
Like morning-suited Witnesses. In wayward ranks around
Her satined feet lounge spikey Gorse and Brambles – finely
dressed
In green and white – her dust-pranked Pages and demure-
faced Maids.
Above all these there glows the proud Groom's iridescent
smile,
Charming his Bride's rich-sparkling jewels into heightened
lights
And coruscating, shimmering, delightful brilliances,
Throughout the tediously long-drawn-out formalities.
Lover of beauty, her handsome Groom, the Sun; and soon
His ardour will strip off that gauzy gown from trembling limbs,
(To consummate his passion, which in him is hotly tensed),
When these elaborate, slow rituals have been dispensed!.

<u>Orphan</u>

Have *you* known the loneliness
    Of a child forlorn?.
Have *you* felt the hopelessness
    Of a child, (rough-torn
From the careful love of mother
And strong shelter of a father),
    Friendlessly withdrawn?.

Some *have* known such loneliness
    Since their first milk-tooth;
They *have* felt that hopelessness,
    Borne the bitter ruth
Of an orphan's constant anguish;
They've *learned* how scorned hearts can languish:
    Torments hard to soothe.

If you have an innocent –
    Whether girl or boy –
Do not let that life be spent
    Other than in joy.
Needless loads of cruel sorrows
Only worsen bleak tomorrows:
    And young lives destroy.

If you know of *any* child
    Suffering despair,
Will you *not* neglect to shield
    But, with loving care,
Lure hope through that hurt heart's rubble?.
Each kind thought helps make dire trouble
    Easier to bear.

Katabatic Kuchina

This raw wind roars and buffets me with rough
And scornful blows from unseen vantage-points.
Exposed, out on a Western hill, I have
Nowhere to hide from these insulting knocks,
But must endure until I can achieve
Some place of shelter from the weather's bane.
    Much as those pale-faced, blindfold prisoners
Once bore the contumelious assaults
Of savage redskin captors, long ago,
Whilst waiting for relieving arrow-barbs
To flense their forfeit lives, (through flesh too flayed
To warrant further degradation there),
Before the gory trophies of their hair, fresh-scalped,
Became adornments for the tribal totem-pole.

Autumnal

I feel Autumnal hints
  Colour the air:
Chamæleonic tints
  Pale-hued and spare.

Bird-clouds traverse the rain-
  Washed, wind-blown skies
As Summer heats decline
  To Winter's ice.

Through failing mortal powers
  I, too, migrate
Across those unknown hours
  Which are my fate.

I trust I shall arrive –
  My transit done –
In some lush Paradise
  Beyond the sun.

Yet, if my hope should be
  Betrayed at last,
All my eternity
  Will be as dust.

But you will never know,
  (Who live distraught
Until *your* time to go),
  My last resort!.

Although Autumnal tones
  Cool my warm breath
I feel, deep in my bones,
  Life transcends death.